# Sugar
# Is
# Sweet

**Other books**

by Gail Kay Haines

*Which Way Is Up?*

by Bruce Hiscock

*Tundra*
*The Big Rock*
*The Big Tree*

# Sugar Is Sweet

## And So Are Lots of Other Things

Gail Kay Haines

*illustrated by* Bruce Hiscock

Atheneum   1992   New York

Maxwell Macmillan Canada
*Toronto*
Maxwell Macmillan International
*New York   Oxford   Singapore   Sydney*

Atheneum
Macmillan Publishing Company
866 Third Avenue
New York, NY 10022

Maxwell Macmillan Canada, Inc.
1200 Eglinton Avenue East
Suite 200
Don Mills, Ontario M3C 3N1

Macmillan Publishing Company is part of the Maxwell Communication Group of Companies.

First edition
Printed in Hong Kong.
1  2  3  4  5  6  7  8  9  10

Library of Congress Cataloging-in-Publication Data

Haines, Gail Kay.
    Sugar is sweet: and so are lots of other things/by Gail Kay
Haines; illustrated by Bruce Hiscock.—1st ed.
    p.    cm.
    Summary: Looks at the reasons why sugar, sweeteners, and all sweet
foods taste good, and explains the role all of them play in people's
diets.
    ISBN 0-689-31723-9
    1. Sugar—Juvenile literature. 2. Sweetness (Taste)—Juvenile
literature. [1. Sugar. 2. Sweetness (Taste)] I. Hiscock, Bruce,
ill. II. Title.
    TP378.2.H35   1992
    613.2.—dc20                                                    91–10606

*To my mother, who loves everything sweet*
*G.K.H.*

*To my nephews, Will and Tom*
*B.H.*

From babies to grandparents, almost everyone loves the taste of something sweet. Apples and candy bars and even diet sodas are popular all around the world. But why do sweet foods taste so good?

Scientists think they know one good reason. Almost all sweet-tasting foods found in nature are safe to eat. Perhaps long-ago humans, living in caves, could tell by the sweetness which fruits and berries were good for their families.

But today, grocery stores are packed with sugary treats, and parents still have to decide which foods are best for their families. Now, some people have the opposite idea. They think all sweetened foods are bad. It's easy to get confused.

Fruit was probably the first "sweet" people ate. Pears, pineapples, and dozens of other fruits all contain a food chemical called "sugar." Sugar makes fruit taste sweet.

Try an experiment. Taste a hard greenish banana and a soft yellow one. Ask someone to put the pieces of banana on a plate for you, so you won't know which is which. Does one taste sweeter? As a banana ripens, it turns other food chemicals into sugar. That's one reason ripe fruit usually tastes sweeter. Try the same test with pears or peaches.

Dried fruit tastes even sweeter than fresh. When the water is removed, all the sugar from a big juicy grape is concentrated in one tiny raisin. Have you ever tasted a dried date? Dates are more than half sugar—as sweet as candy.

About ten thousand years ago, someone discovered the first food sweetener—honey—inside a beehive. No one knew what it was. People guessed that bees collected honey from the sky. They thought it had to be magical, because it tasted so good. Now we know bees make honey from the sugar they find in plants.

Sugar almost always comes from plants—from inside the flowers and the fruits and vegetables. Plants make sugar out of air and water.

Plants act like tiny sugar factories. They take in carbon dioxide from the air (the same gas we breathe out with every breath). They add water from the ground and energy from the sun to build a new chemical—sugar. Then they store it away, for future food.

People in India, thousands of years ago, first grew plants to make sugar. They took the sweet juice from tall sugarcane and dried it into good-tasting brown chunks.

Today, giant factories "refine" the sweet juice from sugarcane or from sugar beets, which grow underground. They clean away all the dirt and other plant parts, until nothing is left but pure sugar. But the factories don't "make" sugar—the living plant does that.

When we say "sugar," we usually mean table sugar—the kind piled in sugar bowls. Its chemical name is sucrose. But sucrose is only one of more than one hundred different chemicals called sugar.

Sugars all contain carbon, the material in pencil lead and charcoal and diamonds. Carbon is a chemical element, made of super-tiny building blocks called atoms. Carbon atoms are a part of every inch of your body, from your hair to your toes to your breath. Chemists label carbon "C."

Sugars also contain water. Water is made from atoms too. Every water molecule contains one atom of oxygen, a gas from the air that we breathe. Every water molecule also has two atoms of hydrogen, another kind of gas. Molecules are groups of atoms, attached together. Chemists call water "$H_2O$."

Foods made from carbon and water are called carbo-hydrates. *Carbo-hydrate* means carbon plus water.

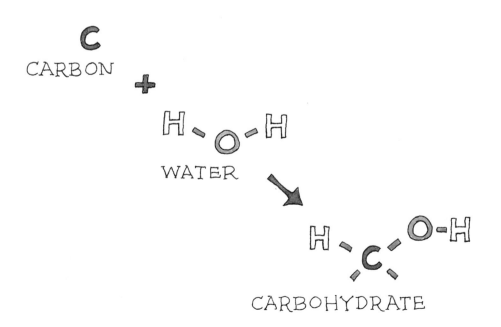

CARBON

+

WATER

CARBOHYDRATE

Food chemists know thousands of kinds of carbohydrates, but the sugars are the simplest ones. Food sugars are made of tiny ring-shaped molecules, much too small to see. It takes billions of molecules to make one crystal of sugar.

Fructose and glucose are two simple sugars you eat every day. Each is made from six carbon atoms and six molecules of water, linked together, but not linked in quite the same way. Nature can build different molecules from the same materials, the way you can build different toys with the same pile of blocks or Legos.

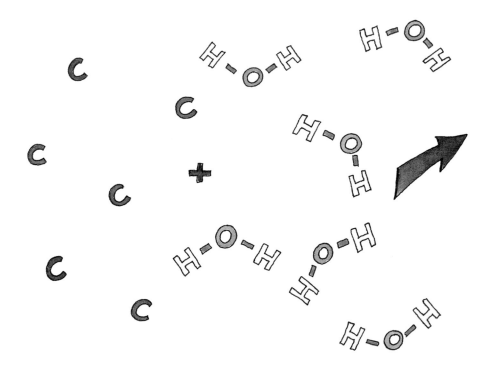

A molecule of fructose is shaped in a five-atom ring. Glucose's ring has six atoms. The other atoms in each molecule stick out in different ways, from the sides.

Sucrose, or table sugar, is made from one glucose and one fructose molecule attached together. It has twelve carbon atoms linked with eleven water molecules. A molecule of sucrose is shaped something like a figure eight.

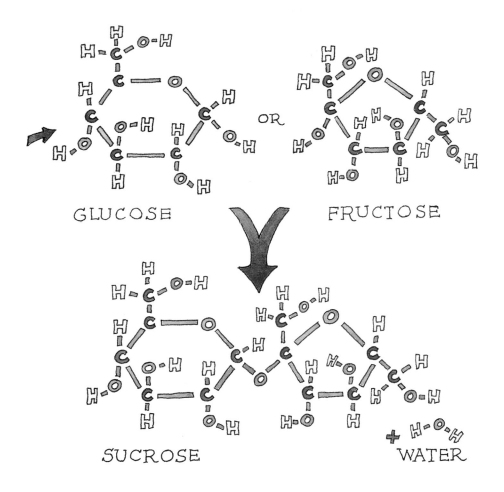

GLUCOSE        OR        FRUCTOSE

SUCROSE                  WATER

When bees make honey, they take sucrose from inside flowers. They split the sucrose into two parts, producing a sticky mixture of fructose and glucose in water.

When you eat sucrose, almost the same thing happens inside your body. Sucrose turns into fructose and glucose.

Fructose is what some people call "fruit sugar," because many fruits make it. You can buy fructose in little packets at the grocery store. Another name chemists use for fructose is levulose.

Some people think fructose is more natural than sucrose. In fact, it isn't. Most fructose sold in stores comes from sucrose molecules that food chemists have split in two. Since fructose is sweeter than sucrose, less is needed to sweeten food.

Try an experiment. Measure a teaspoon of fructose and stir it into a tall glass of ice-cold water. Stir a teaspoonful of sucrose (table sugar) into another glass of ice-cold water. Which tastes sweeter? Now try the same experiment with two cups of hot water. Use half a teaspoon of each this time. Which tastes sweeter? Can you still tell the difference? As fructose gets warm, it loses sweetness.

The other half of sucrose is glucose. Your body uses glucose to carry energy. Glucose is also called corn or grape sugar, because it comes from corn and grapes, or blood sugar, because it flows in everyone's blood. It also comes from other vegetables and fruits. Sometimes chemists call it dextrose.

Glucose is not as sweet as sucrose. That's why corn syrup, a sticky liquid made from corn, is not as sweet as table sugar. Corn syrup also contains a sugar called maltose, which is two glucose molecules attached together. Maltose is only half as sweet as glucose.

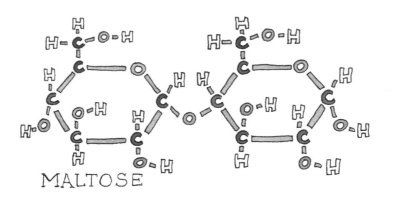

MALTOSE

You can make maltose right inside your own mouth. Take a small bite of bread or potato and suck on it. Try not to swallow. Does it begin to taste a little bit sweet? Saliva turns starchy food into maltose.

Almost every plant on earth makes some sucrose, the most common sugar. Food chemists get sucrose not only from beets and sugarcane but also from grapes and from the sap of maple and palm trees.

Lactose is the chemical name for a sugar in milk. It is formed from one molecule of glucose and one of a sugar called galactose. Since all three are less sweet than sucrose, milk doesn't taste like sugar at all.

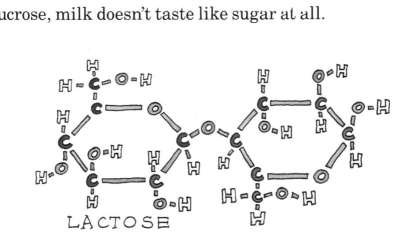

LACTOSE

But why does any kind of sugar taste sweet? What does sweetness mean? Scientists are still trying to find out.

Your tongue has special receptors, or taste buds, for tasting sweetness. It also has receptors for salty and sour and bitter foods. All other flavors are really smells, and you "taste" them through your nose. That's why most foods lose flavor when you have a cold.

Try an experiment. Mix a tablespoon of sugar into half a glass of warm water. Dip a toothpick into the solution and touch it to the back of your tongue. Does it taste sweet? Try the top of your tongue. Each side. Try the tip. Now rinse your mouth and do the same experiment with salty water, with lemon juice (sour), and with strong black coffee (bitter). Rinse your mouth each time. Can you spot some differences?

Receptors can usually recognize more than one of the four flavors, but the strongest sweetness receptors are right at the tip of your tongue. No one knows exactly how they work.

Scientists think what matters most is shape—not the shape of the whole sugar molecule but the way certain atoms stick out from its side. To taste sweet, a sugar molecule must have a three-sided "key" which fits perfectly into a three-sided "hole" on the tongue's receptor. If each corner of the triangle isn't exactly right, the molecule won't taste sweet, just the way a key won't unlock your door if it doesn't fit the keyhole.

Some molecules may have more than one "triangle of sweetness." Maybe the more triangles, the sweeter the sugar. No one knows for sure.

You can spot different sugars in the grocery store by looking at package labels. Most chemical names for sugar end in the letters *ose*. Some ingredients ending in *ol*, such as sorbitol and manitol, are sugar alcohols—slightly different chemicals that also taste sweet. Syrups are sugars too, dissolved in water.

Pick up a box of sweetened cereal and count how many sugars you can find in the list of ingredients. Look at the ingredients of some cookies and granola or breakfast bars. Look at breads and crackers too, and even ketchup. How many can you spot?

Almost every food that comes in a box or bag contains some kind of sweetener. Some have six or more. But does that make a food less good for you? There is no simple answer.

Most people think eating sugar makes them gain weight. It doesn't, any more than any other food. In fact sugar, like all other carbohydrates, is much less fattening than eating butter or the grease on french fries. A teaspoonful of fat has more than twice as many calories as a teaspoonful of sugar.

But sugar causes a special eating problem. It tastes so good people often eat too much. People eat sweets when they aren't even hungry. And many sugary foods, such as cookies and cakes and pies, also contain lots of fattening fat.

As you digest it, sugar provides heat to keep your muscles moving. Sugar has sixteen calories in every teaspoonful, which means your body can burn sixteen calories of energy. But sugar does not supply anything *but* energy—no vitamins or minerals or protein for building strong bodies.

Some people think eating sugar causes them—or their children—to act wild or hyperenergetic. Careful tests done by scientists don't agree. But scientists do agree that eating sugar is not the best way to boost your energy supply. Sugar gives you a quick energy high, like dropping a crumpled ball of paper on a fire. It burns brightly and then is gone.

People also think eating sugar causes their teeth to decay. This is true. But raisins, crackers, fruit juice, and lots of other good foods can be just as harmful to teeth. Even potato chips can cause cavities. Dentists say eating fewer snacks—of any kind—and brushing every time you eat are the key to healthy teeth.

Some people think eating sugar causes diseases, such as diabetes, heart disease, and even cancer. Scientific tests do not agree. But eating sugar can make diabetes— an illness where the body does not produce the right chemicals to digest sucrose—worse.

Some people think one way to cut down on sugar is to use fruit instead. Eating an apple for dessert is a good idea, because it provides other carbohydrates, vitamins, and fiber, along with sucrose, glucose, and fructose.

But eating foods "sweetened with fruit juice; no sugar added," can trick you. They can have more sugar, and more calories, than you think.

Try an experiment. Thaw a can of frozen concentrated apple juice or cider and cook it slowly in a nonstick pan. Use very low heat. Stir often. Add a pinch of cinnamon if you like. In a few hours, you will have a thick, sweet syrup. In another hour or two, you will have a soft, sticky candy, with *no sugar added*. But one tiny spoonful has as much sugar as several whole apples.

To cut down on sugar, some people like to use artificial sweeteners. These are food chemicals that taste sweet—sometimes more than a hundred times as sweet as sugar. You have probably heard some of the names: saccharin, cyclamate, aspartame (Equal or NutraSweet), and ace-sulfame-K (Sunnett).

Artificial sweeteners are so sweet  a tiny pinch can flavor a glass of lemonade or a soft drink. They can take the place of pounds and pounds of sugar, saving thousands and thousands of calories. But every one has some kind of problem.

Saccharin is more than one hundred times as sweet as sugar, but it leaves a bitter taste on your tongue. And some animals that have eaten large amounts of saccharin in safety tests have gotten cancer.

Cyclamate is banned in the United States now, because

some tests showed that it might give cancer to animals. But it is available in Canada and most of the world. It sweetens much less than saccharin, so larger amounts have to be used.

Aspartame is made from two ordinary food chemicals linked together in a new way. It is more than one hundred times as sweet as sugar, and it leaves no bad taste on the tongue. But it comes apart when it is heated, so it can't be used in cookies or cake. There are people who are born with a disorder, called PKU, that makes eating aspartame dangerous. And some tests show it changes the brain chemistry of animals.

Acesulfame-K has been used in other countries for years, but it is new in the United States. It tastes better than saccharin and can stand heat better than aspartame, but scientists still don't know as much about how safe it is.

Almost everyone likes the taste of something sweet. Sugar and other sweet chemicals make foods taste good. But are they good for you?

Try a thinking experiment. Think about a diet of all candy bars and cookies. What about a diet of all pizza or all milk or all broccoli? Now think about a mixture of different kinds of food, including some sweets. You be the judge.

EDUCATION

HF 5986